REFLECTIONS

By Derek Corbally

REFLECTIONS

DEREK CORBALLY

authorHOUSE®

AuthorHouse™
1663 Liberty Drive
Bloomington, IN 47403
www.authorhouse.com
Phone: 1-800-839-8640

First published by AuthorHouse   11/12/2011

ISBN: 978-1-4678-8738-0 (sc)

Printed in the United States of America

Any people depicted in stock imagery provided by Thinkstock are models, and such images are being used for illustrative purposes only.
Certain stock imagery © Thinkstock.

This book is printed on acid-free paper.

Because of the dynamic nature of the Internet, any web addresses or links contained in this book may have changed since publication and may no longer be valid. The views expressed in this work are solely those of the author and do not necessarily reflect the views of the publisher, and the publisher hereby disclaims any responsibility for them.

My intention in publishing this book is not to attack the Church nor the Men and Women that work within the Church, Unless they are evil.

In 1875 in Ireland there were 50 industrial schools. Industrial schools were becoming big business and by 1897 there were 71 schools, of witch 61 (56 schools for Catholics and five for Protestants) Were in the 26 County's.

Priests in Ireland were educated and were nationalistic and regarded as community leaders.

Post-famine records show that the number of Nuns increased eight fold and that there was a huge growth in the number of Priests and Brothers as well as the Nuns.

Moreover, there was even surplus capacity. Many Nuns, Priests and Brothers were exported around the world. Some to do Gods work and some to do the Devils work. All under the flag of the Vatican in Rome.

Protestant Institutions were more richly resourced in Ireland. Thus, a major concern of the Catholic side, witch persisted into the Twentieth century, was to keep Catholic orphans from been taken by Protestant orphan Societies. Overcrowding creating very harsh conditions for the children. Despite this the Church went full steam to obtain orphan children for their Schools and Institutions.

Even back in 1897 the Inspector of Reformatory and Industrial Schools Mr. John Fagan was outraged at the Abuse of Children in the care of the Church and Government. Nothing changed and the suffering continued. www.childabusecommission.ie ... (CICA investigations report)

Ireland was an impoverished country, its people were lacking in education and skills. The poverty line was expanding with great speed through the country. Working the land and the fruits of the land were a lifeline for many to survive the troubled times, Ireland was a third world country.

As in all impoverished countries there are the few that want for nothing and are well off. Among the ranks of the rich there were those who genuinely wanted to help the poor. Some people with foresight saw that education was the way forward and the key to escape poverty for the future.

One of the roles of the institutions and industrial schools was to help educate the youth of Ireland. A large number of these schools were run by the clergy. Christian Brothers only taught young boys. Nuns taught both, although girls were more in number.

Many of these schools and institutions catered for boys and girls for different reasons. Many of these schools received funding from the Government for every child they had on their books.

There were many people who were involved with these schools who were there for genuine unselfish reasons but unfortunately there were many who saw these reform schools and institutions as a way to carry out their sick perverse acts on young children without hindrance. The Church had a very big hold on the poor people of Ireland and because of this and many other reasons many children suffered in silence for fear of not being believed about the atrocities that were taking place at the hands of these evil perverts. Because of this lack of trust in authority, victims remained silent allowing these soldiers of Satan to go unchallenged.

I had the privilege and honour of talking to some survivors of institutions, reform and industrial schools, many said, the schools that they were in as young children were in their eyes the same as the concentration and work camps ,of the Second World War. SS Gestapo officers were of the same mind set as some of the clergy that worked in some of these schools. I can see where these survivors are coming from, comparing the SS Officers and some of the clergy.

As in the death camps and work camps, fear was a dangerous weapon and used at will by those in control. Silence was accepted for one reason or another relating to the mass murder and torture of millions of innocent men, women and children. No one wanted to talk or question the atrocities that took place.

The same can be said for the rape, torture, mental and physical abuse of young children that was taking place within the rank and file of the church within these schools. Many people knew and remained silent; in my mind they too are guilty for their silence. In Ireland there was no fear of been shot for speaking out about the atrocities that were taking place. Damn you for your silence.

No human being anywhere in the world should have to suffer. For some sick reason children's innocence and vulnerability make them easy targets for the sick, evil people of this world.

Many children were sent to these schools and institutions for many reasons, some were sent for not going to school, petty theft, misbehaving and some were just guilty of been wild and hyper children. Some parents just couldn't manage with their large families. I was sent to an orphanage in Dublin despite the fact that my Mother was still alive and well.

There is something that I want to make very clear, not all members of the church were soldiers of Satan, Many were honest, decent, unselfish people who believed in helping the poor and the underprivileged. These honest people I salute.

I believe that despite the revelations relating to the atrocities that took place within the reform schools and intuitions in Ireland, it's only the tip of the iceberg, the worst has yet to be known. The world is a big place and these evil people were sent to all four corners of it.

ME

At the tender age of twelve I was sent to the O.B.I O'Briens Institution Malahide road, Marino Dublin. My Father had just passed away with cancer leaving my wonderful Mother with the hard task of bringing up six young children on her own. Very soon after my Father's death my Mother was approached by a member of the Health Board offering her the opportunity to send me to a boarding school to obtain a better education that would no doubt enable me to have a better future. What Mother would refuse? Little did she know that I was being sent to a living hell. I wonder how many pieces of silver the nurse got. My Mother died from cancer in the year 2000 never knowing what went on in that school and I thank God for that.

Like many victims of any abuse, the hurt, pain, humiliation and guilt that gets buried deep within oneself turns into a cancer and eats away at your mind and soul from within. It seems easier to bury and try to forget than to do battle every day with the worry demons.

When I was twelve or thirteen I was sent from the O.B.I school to St. Kevin's Hospital in Dublin because I was wetting my bed so much. I spent three months in an old mans' ward. I was the only child on the whole landing of the Hospital and I loved it there, I felt safe. I told a Doctor in the Hospital what was happening to me in that school and begged him to keep me in the Hospital; I thought he was a nice man. Nothing was ever done and I was sent back to the school. My bed wetting continued for many years. It was nearly thirty five years before I told another sole anything of my past.

Over the years I tried to live a normal life, I got married to a fabulous girl and had three wonderful sons I had my own business and house.

MY VOLCANO

My volcano was always active although for many years it was in no danger of exploding, although there were some very scary times in my life. One thing that kept me from going over the edge I believe was my writing. I would often wake up in the middle of the night and go for a pen and anything to write on. I found this to be a great release valve. I would write down what was in my head and normally would complete the poem in one go. I very seldom read back over what I had written and when I eventually did for the purpose of this book, I was shocked with some of what I had written. Very little was changed relating to what I had wrote. Spelling and some words were changed in some poems, many are the same as when I first put pen to paper with the exception of the spelling changes.

REASONS FOR THE BOOK

M y intentions with the publication of this book are as follows;
(1) to help other unfortunate victims of abuse. (2) Lend a little
understanding to others, on the ongoing pain and suffering of the
people who were at the mercy of the evil ones. (3) To make my mark
on the rerecords for future generations. (4) Keep exposing the evil
ones and their keepers.

There are many who came forward, your bravery is commendable.
There are many out there who for one reason or another remain
hidden, I understand, that is up to you. Remember that the world is
now aware. Now the survivors can get the help they need, children
can be watched and the evil bastards can be banished and we can get
justice, from God or man

Counselling is a great start to a new beginning. For many years
counselling was not an option for me, my past was my past and not
for another's ears. Why should I trust any person, counsellor or not?
The answer is simple for me, I didn't then and I don't now. I will say
that despite my mistrust with counsellors I found my sessions a great
help regarding moving on with my life and coping with my demons.

A BIT ABOUT: 2009

My writings are somewhat different to what most people would expect poetry to be, and I do agree. Each paper was written as I saw things at that time in my head. Each poem relates to a specific time in my life. At the start of every poem I try to explain where my head was when I was writing. Also where my life was at. Not every event is clear in my head. Some things that happened in my childhood I had forgotten for most of my life. It was only as I started to write things down that memories came back to me and I must say that not all were bad, and I was happy to regain them in my head.

Each poem tells a story and each word has a meaning that may only be explained as you read into each sentence. The poem may also explain itself in verse, or context. To really appreciate each poem and to understand where I was at when writing, maybe you can imagine yourself as a little child of twelve, alone.

I am fifty four years old now, divorced with three wonderful boys. Life is hard, but there are many things I would never change.

ONE

Where was God for me when I was all alone in that school? I begged him to help me but never got help. As far as I was concerned God wanted me to suffer and that is why he never answered my pleas for him to help. I talk about dark cloth with book in hand, they are the clergy. Some were and still are so hypercritical that it's evil. Some are so sick they think they are above the law of the land. They were at one time. Cannon law must allow its members to carry on as they did, otherwise it would have been stopped before the pandemic evil was spread. From all the evidence that is surfacing they knew of the atrocities all along and did nothing to stop it. What was done by the church members will live in the world history books for ever, it will outlast the church, and God will win over evil, always.

God is a bollox, he let me down. He put a thorn in my body from his son's crown.

Calvary was a piece of cake it didn't last too long.

A sheep in dark clothing, the devils long lost son.

Instigators of pain and suffering as sure as the sun.

Green blooded monsters that prey on the young.

Cloaked with dark cloth and book in hand.

A ring of white on the bastards that well understand.

No retribution, a sword in the flesh.

Wounds that remains bleeding until your death.

Internal rotten, a cancer within, destroying innocence step by step.

Calls from hell falling on the deaf.

A crippled body a tortured mind, so well hidden difficult to find.

Every excuse every lie, been a good Father? I got by.

Doing my best while living the lie.

The demons that were planted by gods so called hand are everlasting above this land.

Peace has its time within my mind, it has not come yet I am biding time.

THE WINDOW

I used to stand at the window in my dorm at night waiting to hear the footsteps on the stairs so as I could run back to my bed and pretend I was asleep. At the window I would look out at the world outside and dream. I spent many a night at that window, it was safer there than in my bed. In my bed I could fall asleep and wake up the next morning with wet sheets.

Go beyond the gate beyond the wall.

Standing in a crowded room single and alone, it's nearly dawn.

Subsiding fear the green blooded monster might be gone.

Sleepless thoughts of a life beyond.

A motorbike sounds in the distance night, standing, trembling with no power to fight.

My thoughts are mine, mine to keep. Fear entwining my body from my head to my feet.

The dawn awakes hip hip hooray dry sheets. No vipers tongs today no ridicule or weeps

No need to seek the cage that goes beyond the deep.

Protection not needed, thanks to no sleep.

The day is normal I am one of them, I am six feet tall no need for the pen.

The days are short and the nights are long.

The sun is home bound and is dragging the daylight along.

Sucking on daylight as long as I can, it's fading, night time has just begun.

Darkened clouds roam the night time sky as I stand at my window, a sad little boy.

FOOTSTEPS

Standing at the window I could hear the footsteps from a distance on the bottom of the stairs and I would go back to my bed and pretend I was fast asleep hoping that the green blooded monster was not going to come over to me.

The footsteps are distant, although heavy and loud.

Echoing the hallways like a thundering cloud.

Fear is erupting I am alone.

My body is trembling for fear of the known.

I want to vanish I want to disappear.

The moon has its lights on, footsteps are near.

The light bounces forward, I'll pretend I am dead.

Don't move a muscle, lie still in my bed.

My chest is pounding my fear is growing.

The silence is deafening I am alone.

I long for my Mother and the touch of her hand.

The smell of her perfume, I'm in dream land.

There is movement in the darkness, footsteps are fading away.

I can sleep in my bed tonight, I have wet it anyway.

MAGIC RAIN

There were times I felt dirty and unclean. Not just in my mind but on my body also. To have a dream that could make you free, a magic rain that could wash away everything not good and make you clean in mind and body, what a wonderful thing that would be. No one would be any the wiser that a magic rain made you all new and clean.

The rain is falling it's nice to see, if only it could wash away me.

Fresh new shiny and bright, a magic rain what a delight.

No one would know and no one would see what the wonderful rain has done for me.

Inside out everything clean, New for old and no one has seen.

WHO

An extrovert, I don't think so. I was a good one to hide true feelings. I could hide them so well that no one was ever any the wiser. Someone could crack a joke about abuse, pain or suffering and I could laugh along with it. I became something of an expert in hiding pain within myself. I learned to do this at a very young age; it was a case of having to or suffer things out in the open. Memories or the lack of sometimes hurt the most. Some time I felt that my words hurt my wife and kids, that would cut me up inside and my demons would play havoc with me. I love my family unconditionally and I vowed as a child to protect my children when I had them, I would die without thought for them so any action I took that might have hurt them would eat away at me from the inside. As I say, I was good at hiding it and playing the clown not showing what was behind the mask.

Laughing and joking always having fun, the class clown there is always one.

Hidden thoughts behind the smile, shit in my head that would run for a mile.

C.I.A or K.G.B you wouldn't know it could be me.

Academy awards Oscars who? I don't need one I sure fooled you.

Torture behind the painted face, who do I blame that's not in the race?

Life goes on day by day, demon's feed me thoughts I dare not say.

Smile for the public, bow humble to the meek is there retribution for those I seek?

Old and weary the clown plods on; big shoes funny feet all have fun.

BEAUTIFUL DAY

This poem explains how all hell broke out for me when I would fall asleep at night in my bed in the dormitory and wake up the next morning with my bed wet. The mental torture I had to put up with was very hard. All day I got ridiculed and tormented over wetting my bed. Many of the kids in my dormitory were not my friends and they found life very tough in that school, so it was good for them to have someone to take their frustration out on, unfortunately it was me a lot of the time. Sometimes the Christian Brother would add fuel to the fire of my hell; with his approval I was smelly and unclean to everyone in my dorm.

The sheets are wet what will I do? What will I do? Today, full of ridicule.

Laughs and jokes pushes and shoves, go back asleep pretend you're dead.

The rows awake they'll know I fake; playing dead would be a mistake.

Why the fuck did I not stay awake? The sheets are wet what will I do? What will I do?

The walk of shame as they see the stain, the tap is on to release the pain.

The joke is on me for all to see, if only I could be free.

Wouldn't it be nice to freeze like ice and then no one would know.

Wet or dry I would get by and no stains would ever show.

The sheets are wet what will I do? What will I do?

The boss is here as the sneers disappear; his footsteps are in my line.

Maybe he'll pass to another bed and all will be fine.

Fix the blankets block the stain; it's no good I'm always in the frame.

The sheets are wet what will I do? What will I do?

Pissed the bed again? Echoes the room for all to hear, they again start to sneer.

Blankets are pulled sheets are held, you're a fitly little pup off you go

And wash yourself well.

We don't want our school to smell, the sheets are wet, the sheets are wet.

THE HALL

The hall was great crack. Sliding up and down the halls and corridors of the school with old blankets under your stocking feet, cleaning and polishing as you went along. Everybody that was on that job had fun and we were all of the same mind with no slagging regardless. The floors were that shiny you could see yourself. It was fun especially when it was freezing outside.

Up and down we slide the floors blankets at our feet.

Shine reflecting ceilings high everything so neat.

Work is fun for everyone with blankets at their feet.

Up and down round and round, having fun without a sound.

Shining, cleaning, and polishing all as we slide up and down the hall.

Smelly socks we have none as we slide and have some fun.

MIRROR FACE

I was always thinking, could people read me and did they know what was going on in my head. I wasn't happy with a lot of my life and I believed that sometimes, depending were my head was at, people could look into my face and know my thoughts. I taught myself to read and write. I hated school and never trusted any teacher. For self-preservation I blanked out parts of my childhood. In doing so I probably lost good memories from that time.

Is it me or can people see what's behind the door?

Mirrored face not to be seen, who am I? Am I clean?

Mirrored face not to be seen, was it something I done?

Am I not good, banned from fun?

Where are my memories, thoughts and time, were has it all gone?

Mirrored face I've lost the race, frozen on the starting line.

They have passed me by every last one, all smiling having fun.

Is it me? Can people see what's behind the door?

Empty, lost, cold as stone, blood of green, all alone.

SLEEP OVER

Sleeping over, never happened. Wetting my bed was one thing but to wet a bed in my friend's house or anywhere, unthinkable. My bedwetting secrets were left in the OBI school and in my head and that's where I wanted them to stay. I don't think that I could live with the stigma of wetting my bed where I lived and had all my friends. Can you imagine my mate's slagging me, the grief of the past it would open up again?

You must be joking it can't be true, hold your breath try turning blue.

The fire is burning it won't go out, run outside let your body shout.

They won't believe there will be doubt.

Happy days they lie ahead, I don't believe no more wetting the bed.

Wishful thinking I wish it were true, my thoughts are changing what will I do?

I'm getting older I can't sleep out, my friend's Mother will start to shout.

Secrets, secrets I have them all, much too heavy I am starting to fall.

Better not to explain, invited doubt becomes more pain.

Maybe someday I will be free, time will tell.

Let's just wait and see.

DEMONS PARTY

Memories from the OBI school and all the guilt and questions that came from my stay in that Hell. Why was I in that school? Why was I left there? Were the fuck was God and his almighty power? I always had a fear of information getting out of what went on in that school so I never asked any questions for fear of the answers and the possibility of a chain reaction with the questions. It was much easier to bury any questions with my past.

Torment is resident in my head I get no peace in my bed.

Demons party without song never invites me to go along.

Day or night they play a game; it's never fun it's full of shame.

Secrets many we can tell revealed I call the train to hell.

Adjust with the time, learn the game learn to mime.

Silence is a golden rule to my memories from that school.

Reveal one reveal all put them on a market stall.

Everyone can see the glass that will bring them to my past.

Like a bird in a cage released to freedom, die or be saved.

SNOW DROP

WHAT CAN I SAY, I have experienced three snow drops first hand and what a wonderful experience for any Father. The birth of a child has got to be in my book the most wonderful miracle that has ever been known to man. A true account of the might of Gods power. A magical gift to parents.

A newborn child is a wonderful thing enough to make the angels sing.

Heavens gates will drop a cloud and in its mist a baby is found

Shining gleaming white as snow a wonderful mystery starts to unfold.

A new beginning with the first breath that will last until its death.

THE DORM

There were nights that I would lay in my bed in the dormitory afraid to go to sleep for fear I would wake up the next morning with my bed wet. Sometimes as I lay in my bed, my mind would wander and I would dream. Other times I would look around the room and pick things in the room to play a game in my head. Nearly every time my eyes were drawn to the doors that divided the hall from the dormitory. I would look so hard that I imagined the doors laughing at me and making faces, scary shit for a child. It was what came through them doors I feared.

Close the door turn off the light the day is past its time for night.

Time to look time to dream, beyond the walls beyond the view
Before the evil comes for you.

Unclosed doors are always there, laughing at you, inviting fear.

Close your eyes disappear, a magic wand dissolve the spell, salvation from hell.

MOTHER

All Mothers have a special bond with their children and have a little something extra for them they feel might need it. For my Mother to lose her Father at a very young age and then lose her Mother was very hard on her. To have her husband die early in their marriage certainly had taken its toll on her. To lose a son and never have the opportunity to have a funeral and say her good buys to him and finalize things is unthinkable. It created demons from hell to torment her life. Her kingdom was her family. With a soft tone in her voice she only had to say things one time. She liked things as there were, if it wasn't broken then don't fix it was her line of thought. When I got the phone call to say she had passed away I knew then her torment and pain had ended. She was at peace and reunited with them that went before her. I would have loved to be with her holding her soft gentle hand as she passed over, I missed that and I miss her very much.

I miss the smile the gentle hand.
A comforting prescient, her firm stands.
The command of a general, a will with power.
The face of an angle, I missed the hour.
With a love for her space and little change
Her kingdom was close at hand.
A treacherous road and a difficulty past, Freedom called at last.
A heavy heart and a burdened mind a life she knew so well.
Dreams of the imposable, always onward bound.
A faith of stone for the prodigal son.
A wish unfulfilled for his return.
A cold reality time to let go, united.

ELEPHANT

When I lost my temper I really lost it I was a very different person. I would break things and shout very loud and say hurtful things, a bully to the core. I was a very vindictive person when I was in a rage. When I broke things in the house, it was always things that meant something special. I would replace them but it was never the same, the replaced items became reminders of the bad me, a reminder to punish myself and a reminder to release the guilt demons. I could never understand why I lost it and that would eat me up even more inside. I always felt sick for doing what I did and remorse was a demon that had a feast after the event, especially if the kids heard or saw what was going on. Is it any wonder my marriage went to the wall. I wouldn't have stayed with me.

Anger and strife take it out on the wife and all that's around.

Turn the music high and blank all other sound.

Friends calling don't answer, pretend you're not there.

There only here to nose they don't really care.

Head is pounding blood is high

Volcano is bubbling don't know why.

Body's hyper thoughts are fast, not one memory of the past.

Head is melting no reason why, thoughts of death I want to die.

I did it again as in the past; pressure is building how long will it last?

I promised myself never again

House is silent not empty, alone again.

AS GOD INTENDED

I saw two young children playing in the botanic Gardens in Dublin on a fine summer's day. They played among themselves as if the rest of the world didn't exist, and they were oblivious to all around them. Two men of the cloth strolled by talking to each other. From the time of their approach until they passed the Mother scanned the two men with the corner of her eye. I wondered if that young Mother had a bad experience with the people of the cloth or was it just motherly instinct to sense danger. God intended all children to have innocence and enjoy their childhood.

They are happy; their laughing it's great to see.

I wonder if they have thoughts like me.

There all together having fun I wonder if I am the only one.

Moving unseen within a crowd children playing laughing out loud.

Mother scans with a watchful eye as muzzled dogs slowly pass them by.

Life is wonderful life is gay, danger oblivious as they play

Open and pure within the day

Children, as God intended, innocent within their play.

LITTLE CHILDERN

M any years have passed for them that are still alive who were in some sort of institution or reform school run by members of the cloth (Clergy). I had the privilege of been sent to an institution for orphans and I still with a Mother. Numbers were important for many institutions as they received payment from the Irish Government for each child they on their books. As people who were in these places got older and there demons got out of hand, information started to leak out regarding what went on in the schools and institutions. Understandably the reports that were coming to the authority were beyond belief. As time went on more victims of the rape, abuse and torture came forward and the powers that be could not ignore or hide their stories anymore. Many people had buried very deep their past and with all the media attention, it released their demons again. As many of us did in the past we adapted, it was time to do it again.

There here there everywhere memory's of the past
I knew it was too good to be true I knew it wouldn't last,
Buried underneath the grave deep within the ground
Hidden for such a long time never to be found.
Moving like a heavy storm across the land, people started
Talking trying to understand.
Evil in abundance the devil with both hands
How could this have happened in this small land?
Hardship, pain and suffering brought by an evil hand.

Suffer ye little children suffer ye on this land.

Put into the hands of evil sent through the gates of hell.

Suffer you little children and secrets never tell.

Rape, abuse and torture all you'll ever know

Memory that will stay with you and love will never show.

Now the coffin is lifted and secrets they are seen

People can but wonder what evil has there been.

DARK CLOTH

This one speaks for its self; they will have to stand before God almighty on judgment day from the pope down.

The devil he lived in Ireland and ruled with an evil hand

He sacrificed the vulnerable that could not make a stand.

He used his troop of dark cloth, some with collars shining white

To crush the young and pure and scar them all for life.

His subtle way of moving across our green land, ripping out the

Hearts of the young, that couldn't make a stand.

Knowing or unknowing to the powers that be,

Evil ruled for all, with the good book to see

No one ever taking a stand, to rid this evil from our land.

When perversion exceeded expectations and got totally out of hand

The evil bastards were rewarded with new victims and sent to another land.

WORDS

Words were a sword with me I could cut a tree in half with them. My ex wife said to me one time that some of the things I said to her ,were a lot worse than if I had hit her. If you don't mean it don't say it

Words there all mixed up in my head, I'm not sure what I said.

Hurtful and stabbing tones not intended, true colour not shown.

Always feelings of remorse, static let things take their course.

No need to explain, tears hidden by the pain.

Chipping away at the hearts shell, untold damage with words I cannot spell.

Watering seeds of mistrust, exposing love to the worst.

Always sadness always remorse, letting the outcome take its course.

Always present always there, deepening shadows create a scare.

Mixed words that don't belong, throwing them out with random shout

Always feeding the seeds of doubt.

WHITE WORDS

Words can be a dangerous sword.

If you don't mean it don't say it

White words quickly turning black, throwing them out returning back.

Never known what was said, always returning to the bed.

Speeding thoughts going through your head, analyzing what was said.

The room is closing the space is tight, walking the dark without a light.

White words that were sound now are nowhere to be found.

Mixed up, confused no to go, black words humming starting to glow.

Asking them to go away with options to come back another day.

Any compromise that will rest your eyes.

Sleep, what a surprise.

STARS

Standing at the window in my dorm at night became the norm for me and was a very important space. I had a few safe places in that school. Places that offered me different sanctuary's and my window offered me early warning to the danger that the night could bring. My window was a place to dream and use my imagination and ask questions. A place of hope.

The stars are many out to night; I look and like to see their light.

I try to count but lose my place; I see the glass then see my face.

I have a nose two ears a mouth; I open wide but dare not shout.

Reflection, who am I? Can you take me to the sky?

Silence, we still have time to play a game that's only mine.

Many faces in the glass waiting for the time to pass.

Who put the stars in the sky out of reach and very high?

Who turns them out when the daylight is here?

Do stars ever cry? Do they have fear? Reflections why so sad?

The games are good that we have. Wipe away your little tear

Talk to the stars, they will bring you cheer.

DOCTOR, DOCTOR

At some stage in my stay at the OBI school somebody, I still don't know who decided to send me to St James Hospital in Dublin city to see if they could determine what was causing my bed wetting and fix it. I think the decision came after I was found asleep at the window with my pyjamas wet, at least my bed was dry. I was put in a ward in the hospital with only old men with tubes out there sides and a bag of piss strapped to them most of the time. At first the whole situation was very daunting as you can imagine for a child of 12. I soon adapted and it became my safe place of all time. All my praying and begging with God had finally paid off, I was free and safe. I felt that safe there I told a doctor what was happening to me in the school. I don't know how long I was in the Hospital but I was devastated when they sent me back to the OBI Institution. (I stayed in the Hospital for three months, Records Dep. St Kevin's Hospital Dublin.)

Doctor Doctor let me stay; don't send me back to that place.

I love it here I'm having fun I'm making friends with everyone.

They're all very old but I don't mind they give me sweets of every kind.

I miss them when they pass away, sometimes one sometimes two a day.

I ask for them and I am told, they're gone to heaven, they were old.

They're happy now with no more pain in the house of God.

When you get old you'll do the same, now run along like a good little lad.

I love this place it's so much fun, adventures, everyday has one.

Family comes to see I'm well I'm, in heaven removed from hell.

I've made a new friend he's young like me and he wets the bed for all to see.

He laughs and jokes and doesn't care and never seems to have a fear.

Doctor, Doctor please let me stay don't send me back to that place.

SECRETS

We all have something in our lives that we want to keep deep within ourselves despite the consequence to our mind and body and those around us. We learn to cope as if it is not there within us and we know nothing of it. There are times when we long to share the secrets with someone but we don't stop to do so, we keep moving with life as it is, with no change in pace so as not to let anyone know that there might be something wrong with your life that needs outside help. I sometimes thought to end it all, everything, my life. To close the book and make the demons homeless. You never will, there is some sort of strange comfort in thinking about it though. It feels good to have complete control over something, even if it's your life. You know deep down that you will never close the book and make the demons homeless despite all, you have too much around you to lose.

You play the game and carry on, pretending to have fun

You keep your smile and walk the mile, never stop or never run

You keep the pace and no one knows, that you're bleeding deep inside

Life goes on . . . Pain lets you know you're still alive

To everyone your doing well and always on the move

You never want things to end, although you think and do pretend

You've got too much to lose

No one must know the way you think, they'll see you lost your end

You carry on with your life, Pretend, pretend, pretend.

LO

I was married for twenty seven years I am now divorced. I hear men in my situation talking about their ex wife's with evil in there tone. They see their past life as a total waste and missed opportunity and don't seem to have a good word for the ex lover. I hear them say how they went beyond the call of duty in their marriage. Looking back on time over the last twenty seven years there are some things I would change if given the chance again but for the most of it I would not change a thing. Even the hard times and there were many. We had fun and were united as a family as we knew it. I could not have asked for a better woman to rear and prepare our three children for the world. Despite the lack of knowledge in bringing up children and my wife being so young, she did everything any child expert would recommend. I always said it and I will say it again, she was our rock. There is one thing I can be very sure of; I will never be one of the sad people I talked about above.

The sun is not always shining nor would I expect it to

I had some wonderful times in life and those times were spent with you.

We laughed and cried together as moments were made in the past.

Those moments became memories and memories will always last

No need for video or photos there all within my head and can

Easily be summoned to come to life, especially as I rest my head.

Three strong young children made us proud as proud could be

The fact of their existences, they will live for eternity.

SOLDIERS OF EVIL

Evil is everywhere the good book says and we must be vigilant and strong to steer clear of it. When the very people who are servants of God and teachers of his divine word are the very ones that are evil then it becomes very difficult to note evil. The word of God talks about us being aware of the wolf in sheep's clothing, why did God not put it a little more simple and tell us that they could be dressed in dark cloth with white collars, it would have made things a little easier and may have saved a lot of lives from the demon's of the devil. Take note that these solders of evil are dressed in plain clothes also. I long for the day that I will stand with God and point the finger because I don't think there will be real justice on this earth.

You put your hand inside my flesh and ripped away my heart.

You left me with a longing from the very start

A child was I of innocent mind with dreams to fulfil

You planted the seed of torment and took away my will

You made me vow a silence to last my whole life long

It was easier to forget, it helped me carry on

Now that I am older things I understand, you are a solider

Of the devil and under his command

Your task, destroy the innocent and make their souls unclean

And live a life of secrets that will shatter any dream.

You underestimated the power of the almighty, the creator of this land

I took strength from his son's persecution, power from his bloodstained hands.

I stand accuser before you with God at my side, Get thee behind me Satan

The Church has surely lied. It covered for the evil of men with collars shining white,

I now have strength to carry on and live a normal life . . . .

BURNING INSIDE

Despite all that happened in my life I tried to adapt and carry on as best I could. There were times I found it very difficult coping with my life. Meeting Lo (my wife) was a new beginning for me. The start to a new life and when my three children arrived into our lives the Heavens needed thanking. The wonderful memories of growing up with my children are engraved in my mind. I can call on memories and do, to help me through bad times. I often lie on my bed and open my good memory box and I am at peace.

Older now with bad memories of the past, it's amazing how these thoughts last.

Through time and strife three children a wife, the burning is still the same.

Keeping it all to myself packed away neatly on the shelf, you learn to play the game.

There are things I will never change they brought me so much joy

They gave me strength to carry on when I felt I wanted to die.

New memories were made by the minute with the birth of each new Son.

The joy and love they gave to me is what made me carry on.

A woman that I cherish always a rock to lean upon

A blessing from the heavens, my light from the sun.

Looking back on happy memories that help fill my mind,

Wonderful times that have been, now imbedded in my mind.

JUDGMENT DAY

Now that I am older and no wiser as to why so many evil people found the Church a safe place to be and carry out the work of the devil. I have often wondered how these evil people could do what they did to little children and go unnoticed by their superiors. Maybe they didn't go unnoticed then they too are guilty. The damage that was done to people's lives is well beyond belief and leaves what was done in some work camps by the sick Nazis similar. The seeds of pain that were planted into children and watered by Priests, Christian brothers, Nuns and lay people when manifested, they released the devils own word that will carry on within people's minds and souls for generations to come, the word of evil. I dread to think of the children that were raped, tortured and abused in these schools and institutions where are they are today. Alcoholism, drug addiction, mental disorders and so on are all the manifestations of the evil that was inflicted on the young children, evil that was inflicted on these young children are passed through to their families so they too can suffer. The devils work can go on and on for generations to come, nice one Mr. Christianity

You made the evil monsters to scourge and torment this earth
You made them sick in mind they are the walking dead
You gave them positions of authority with power at their hand
To strike out and destroy children upon this so call holy land
They were given freedom from prosecution no matter what they done
They called themselves Christians, followers of Gods only begotten son

They are the hand of evil, even the blind can see

Why did they let this happen? To children o so sweet

Taking away their little hearts for these so call guardians to eat

They thrive upon the innocent flesh with torture, suffering and pain

Why did they let this happen in Gods holy name?

Is it part of a teaching that no one took a stand against this unholy evil?

That covered our holy land.

These people went unpunished for evils of the devils hand,

They were rewarded and sent to another land.

To carry out the torture, suffering and pain.

The powers that be were in denial and took a protective stand they are

Guilty as the guilty, for evils that were done.

When the Lord returns to earth their judgment day will come.

COLLARS OF WHITE

One always felt alone and isolated.

Before all the very brave people came out and told the world what the church and its members had done to them, many secrets were kept inside. People would have loved to shout at the top of their voice and release all the secrets that were chained inside them for years. I assume that if given the chance to rid the sick, evil, perverted solders of evil from this our land and banish them to the deepest and darkest pits in hell they would do it without hesitation. Until recent years you stood alone with technology and education, we are no longer standing alone. The world knows something of what went on and the effects the Abuse had on our lives and our wives and children, Family and friends. I have no doubt that there will be a lot of research done in this area in the future and will be on the record books for ever. So I no longer stand with my feet tied to my hands and my mouth gagged.

You stand alone from a distant crowed; you want to shout but are not allowed

Your hands are tied to your feet; your half naked body is half covered with a white sheet

You wish that you could make a stand and clear these people from the land

They all dressed with dark cloth of heavy might and some with collars shining o so white

You wish that you could make a stand and clear these people from the land

They stand all ranks firm in hand, with no respect for God or man

Denying all troubles told, protecting evils that are old

God with his almighty hand will banish this evil from our land

Now I do not stand alone I stand beside Gods almighty throne

Now the stories can be told and rid this evil that is old.

OSTRAGE

E ven to this day after the Irish Government commissioned a report (the Ryan report 09) into the Rape, Torture and Abuse at the hands of these people in Reform schools and Institutions in Ireland only, the powers of the church still stood in denial as to the extent of the abuse that took place, and its scale. Ireland is only the tip of the iceberg in relation to the extent of the abuse that Priests, Christian brothers, nuns and lay people are responsible for around the world, and I firmly believe this. I think that it is the responsibility of the Roman Catholic Church to pay full costs of an independent body to be set up to investigate worldwide possibilities of abuse by its members. Abuse been denied or sidetracked by the church from the Pope down. It only highlights to everyone just how far from the Word of God the church has strayed in relation to its views of child torture and the truth.

The cloud is lifted it's not the same, why do they want to play this game

To carry on causing pain, not listening and doing the same

It's in the open for all to see, it's not just one it's not just me

Why do the play this hurtful game?

Causing survivors much more pain.

DANCING WITH CLOWNS

It's not very difficult to pretend to others that all is fine and that you are getting on with life the same as everyone else. Sometimes other people looking at you would easily assume that you are doing well in life and don't seem to have the problems and pressures that they have. I was always one to have more than one iron in the fire and had no trouble taking a chance. Creating an image was never done with the slightest intent to be bad to anyone. They could not see the real situation in my life. If I had small money and not enough to pay all the household bills and needed a break then I would pay no one and take the break. To everyone looking on I was doing very well in life.

You might be right in thinking; I'm not all together there

Sometimes by my action you would think I didn't care

I often throw caution to the wind and not bother to put up my sails

I drift along behind the breeze with the world between my knees

Some say that I'm a dreamer, with my head above the clouds

Living life and having fun while dancing with the clowns.

Mr. happy go lucky with not a care in the world

Not the slightest weight on my shoulders, not a burden to be had.

Everyday looks wonderful and pleasant to the eye

It would seem that my life, is always filled with joy

It's easy to pretend, it's easy to live the lie.

WALKING

Walking was always a great way for me to clear my head. I didn't really care where I went as long as I was walking. It was never power walking so I never lost Weight but I had strong legs and a flat bum. I have often been able to sort out things in my head when walking when there seemed no solution. Walking in the rain is also a great way to release excess steam. There is something of a good feeling, walking and crying, it has to be raining of course.

Walking, walking anywhere, what direction I don't care

Sun, rain, hail or snow put my shoes on and off I go.

Walking helps me clear my mind and find solutions I couldn't find

It lets me cry when in the rain, no one sees that I'm in pain

What direction I don't care, my walking shoes take me anywhere

I like to do it when alone, walking in my safety zone, in the crowds but still alone.

I see the clouds I see the trees, I feel the comfort of a summer breeze

Winters chills warm my face keep my step and keep my pace.

Home again and feeling good, happy with the route I took.

Tomorrow brings another day; again my feet will have to pay.

TOLL

For a long time I was asking myself why did I not run away from the school or tell someone in the school what was going on. It was only in later years that I suddenly realized that I was only twelve years old. A child of twelve in 2010 and a child of twelve 1979 are very different. Computers, mobile phones, freedom from the church, It was a very different time. I talk about the toll and I paid this one dearly. Carrying the baggage from the past was a cancer within me and corroded the very body that was the prison cell for my secrets. Today I am a little free that some of the demons are out. Counselling is a must no matter what you think. I never thought that I would ever speak to someone I didn't know from Adam and tell them things that were troubling me.

I should have seen it coming; surely there was something I could have done?

Why did I stand frozen? Why did I not run?

Surely someone would have listened to what I had to say?

Did I allow this to happen? Is that why I have to pay?

I tried to tell a Doctor who I thought was a good man

I told him what was happening and released the secrets from the can.

Nothing ever happened things remained the same, he sent me

Back to that school with new guilt and shame.

I never told another for fear of what they would say I carried the demons

Deep inside until this very day.

Forty years have gone away and the demons have had their toll

I've carried this can of secrets to long; I am now getting so old

This can is old and battered, secrets no longer can it hold

I've learned to talk with people good, secrets they can unfold

They do believe and understand the toll I had to pay, and

It's what, keeps me going to this very day.

NOVIS

I cannot say for sure and only guess what kind of conversation went on when a senior brother was teaching a trainee Christian Brother on the way to deal with young children under his care in the reform schools and Institutions. I base my assumption on the evidence that is public knowledge and from my personal experiences with the Christian brothers. There is no way that there could be so many sadists and sick people that just arrived at the doors of the Christian brothers teaching school looking to start work, raping, torturing and abusing young children. So with that assumption I will guess that some were taught what to do.

It never happened; those brats are full of lies

They're evil ungrateful with no respect inside

They need to learn a lesson, a hard one they'll understand

One they won't forget in a hurry, start with the leather strap in your hand.

Use it with power and might, make sure it leaves a mark.

If it doesn't work in daylight then use it in the dark.

Remember, they are social degenerates, unholy for this land

Sent to us for converting, they need to understand.

The law of the church is not questionable by any ungowned man.

Do what you see fit to make them understand.

Suffering and pain is a gift for them, so give it with clear mind.

Your reward will come on judgment day when the converted are at your side.

Force and power is needed to drive there evil out.

Do not let the fact that they are so young, create any doubt.

Pay no head to their screams; it's the devil that you hear,

Keep the word of God at hand and walk without tear.

ANOTHERS SIN

I carried the can for years thinking that it was mine to carry, it was not. It belonged to another.

Why does it happen just to me?

Am I not good for the entire world to see?

Am I destined to carry this shame?

Is my life's purpose to play this game?

I go along every day, with thoughts in my mind I cannot say

People I see do not understand, why I carry life with such a heavy hand

Buried deep love that cannot get out, held down with secrets I cannot shout.

Living a life deep from within, tormented for another's sin

Words of wisdom crash my mind, to take my past and leave it behind

Memories that I cannot shout, trail my life with constant doubt

A future that I cannot see, life without guilt will set me free.

THE BEACH

Walking beside the sea on the beach is pleasant to do at any time of the year. Each season has its own beauty and character. There is a magic all on its own when you let it happen and you are alone, well you think you are.

I like to walk on the beach, with the sand O so soft at my feet
The distant ship beyond the wave, the birds that nest above the cave
The clouds that roll across the sky, the gentle wind that passes by
A whisper of a hidden past of ships long ago, that was lost
Tales buried within the deep, a treasure chest the sea must keep.

PRESIOUS STONE

Sometimes you do not realize just how precious a stone you have until you don't have it anymore. That's the way I feel about my partner of twenty seven years. Life moves on and you learn to adapt very fast or you live in the past and you die inside. It's time to make new memories.

I've lost a gem in the mist; I thought was clinched within my fist

Precious as precious stones can be it slipped and got away from me

My loss brought me totally down, nearly two where the stone was first found

It took me time to carry on; with no stone there was no sparkle from the sun

Time crawled forward with memories hard, a vital organ tore apart

Waiting time to carry on and getting that sparkle from the sun.

GASTAPO

have absolutely no problem comparing some members of the cloth to the SS of the last world war. I talk about times in the OBI Institutions Dublin. Their presents created fear. Freedom was just out on the other side of a gate and yet very few took it. Fear ran the school with bullies to oversee. That school at times made that you wanted to die. They removed your will and your soul and in doing so they took away all dreams that a child should have. Part of their job in that school was to make you forget that you were human, a person.

Gestapo dressed in black and white, there sudden presents create a fright

Fear is rampant right throughout a happy life is always in doubt

Freedom, just beyond the wall beyond the gate, a life without fear a life without hate.

Statues that stare within the night, creating shadows creating fright

Little feet running around, Gestapo standing their ground

Ruling with an iron hand, little children working the land.

Singing songs you don't understand, chanting words from another land.

Eating bread from that evil hand, while surrounded by hypocrites, told where to stand.

Dreams of a future that may never come, wishing your life away before it's begun.

Damage inside you cannot repair, caused by people that just didn't care.

Disbelief clouds your mind from things you see

A little older now realizing you're a human being

Life's paths are many, confused with choice, fears of the freedom you longed all your life.

Steel walls that were built within, placed by evil to prevent sin

Love is a word you don't understand, extinguished by the Gestapo's righteous hand.

FAMILY

In this poem I talk about what I had regarding family life. Watching the kids growing up and watching them become young men. Our marriage break-up has had some sort of a negative impact on the kids, it had to have had. We tried very hard to lessen the impact it was going to have on them. We all seemed to go different ways for a time. I think the reason we all came back together in a different way was that we all missed the Family as a unit and all that goes with it. We have always held onto the love that we have for each other. We are still a very close family unit just in a different way now.

Fifty today looking back on time, I've lost so much that I thought was mine

Memories I have bitter and sweet, I thought I had the world at my feet

It's all gone away and so much has changed, Was it me that broke the frame?

A family united steadfast to the core, A family united we are no more.

I long for the comfort of our family touch, the laughter and arguing I miss so much

A lesson hard learned with time gone by, Everyone's dreams throwing up in the sky

Seeds that were planted in happier times, Starting to bloom creating sound minds

Children becoming men with the world at their feet, their lives again looking O so neat

Taking separate roads with new goals in mind, but having held on to memories from behind

Now we laugh and joke of times gone by, All our dreams are touchable we are again in the sky

United, happy and having fun, with love in our hearts, everyone

It's not the same as it was before, these time the ships a little from the shore . . . .

REDRESS

This poem I had to add to the book. I just cannot believe that with all the revelations of the past regarding the Rape, torture and abuse of little children by the members of the Roman Catholic Church that they still are playing the torture game with the survivors of abuse.

It proves to me that the Church is still playing the ostrich regarding the abuse within its rank and file. One must ask the questions, why are they doing this? What are they trying to cover up now?

Redress, Dance in the puddles of pain and cause more stress.

Ask perverted questions, justify your seat

Box pain and suffering, make everything look neat.

Cheep trills that pay your bill for the sick behind the mask.

Pretend you understand the pain of the survivors who make a stand.

Go with the flow; don't let the shine on your arse show.

Box it all off then place the bow, another one bites the dust not many to go.

Legal eagles, Academics that can't use a phone

Numbers not faces, true suffering unknown.

Drag it out play the game, another raisin for the scone.

Men of black now wear the sack hiding there white collars of shame.

There higher power again denying the hour and playing the numbers that they stained.

There thoughts infested with demons of old, there Church of comfort littered with gold.

Distort the truth play it down, laugh at the man with thorns for a crown.

THE FINAL STRAW

In recent years very brave people decided to take a stand against the religious orders and its members. The church leaders ignored cries for justice and help by the victims of abuse, rape and torture. Because of their stand it became impossible for Religious Authorities and the Government to ignore what these people had to say. They could no longer play 'the ostrich' and bury there devious heads in the sand. Due to the sick nature of the information that was coming to light, the Government had no choice but to set up a commission to investigate the growing number of complaints relating to unbelievable accounts of rape, torture, mental and physical abuse within the Religious institutions and schools in Ireland.

The Ryan Report was set up and its findings, regarding the atrocities that took place on young children, boys and girls, within the Religious organizations and institutions shocked and sickened the Irish people. As the devilish deeds that took place on the young children began to emerge, world media covered the stories. This time the Church, Government and An Garda Siochana (Police) could not cover up and hide the truths that were emerging about the rank and file of the Church. Evidence revealed atrocities by the clergy on young children that shock and sicken the world. Perverted members of the cloth, who raped, tortured and abused young children and went unpunished for years. Not alone did the evil clergy go unpunished, many were rewarded by the church for doing the work of the devil and sent to destroy the lives of more young children around the world. They have yet to stand up and be counted.

The Murphy Report for the Dublin atrocities revealed further truths that shocked the world.

Cover ups, perversion, paedophilia on a massive scale within the rank and file of the church.

The poems in this book are from a survivor of the evil side of the church.

Each poem when written was a form of therapy. It is a little look into the mind of a survivor and his life. I hope that in some small way this book has helped you understand what went on within the Church in Ireland and around the world.

The worst has yet to come.

A special thanks to Sengmany Chanthalangsone for her understanding and friendship.

To my ex-wife Lo, have a wonderful life you deserve it. To my three Sons, a big thank you for being yourselves.

Thanks to the people at AuthorHouse Publishing for your professional support.

I am not going to list any help line information, different strokes for different folks. There are plenty of good people that will help you when asked. Don't be shy they have heard it all before.

The way is open for a helping hand; don't let your thoughts weaken your stand.

Walk towards you fear with mighty power armed with that knowledge, you cease the hour.

Keep your head way up high; let others demons pass you by.

Wash in the water that makes you clean, turn on the tap you have not seen.

You have that power to change your life and rid yourself of the demons light.

The world will be a sadder place, if someone has to take your space.

Ryan Report Ireland. ie

Murphy Report Ireland. ie

Dublin church report. ie

Garda report into church sex abuse. ie

Church sex cover-ups. ie